THE
EARTH

One-of-a-Kind Planet

LAURA PERDEW

Illustrated by Shululu

A long, long time ago, Earth was lifeless. Hot, gassy, bubbly. But then . . . it cooled—slowly—slowly—slowly—slowly. Water collected. Itty-bitty, teeny-tiny life forms emerged. And now, Earth is full of life. Then, new life produced oxygen—which built up in the atmosphere.

Hello, Earthling!

I'm Universe, and I'm here to tell you about some of my best parts, like your amazing planet, Earth. It's my pride and joy. You live on Earth, but do you know how incredible it really is?

Oh boy, here we go.

Yup. Universe is bragging about Earth again.

1

Let's start with its solar system.
There are eight planets there!

Earth is the third planet from the sun. And
each of the planets—including yours—
orbits around the sun on its own path.

**It's a pretty neat system,
if I do say so myself.**

MARS

MERCURY

EARTH

VENUS

Do you know how long your planet has been part of that system? Earth has celebrated more than

4 billion, 500 million birthdays!

When Earth was first born, it was a
hot,
 bubbling,
  gassy mess for a
   VERY long time.

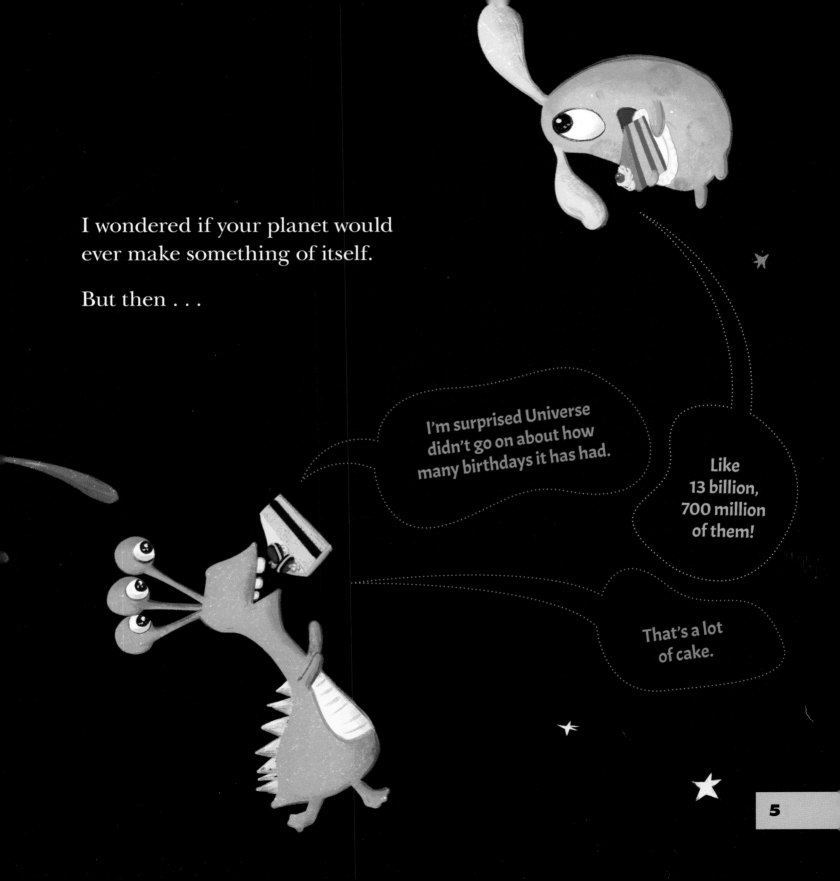

I wondered if your planet would ever make something of itself.

But then . . .

I'm surprised Universe didn't go on about how many birthdays it has had.

Like 13 billion, 700 million of them!

That's a lot of cake.

5

. . . slowly . . . slowly . . . **sloooooooooowly,** it cooled.

It's still pretty hot on the inside, even today.
And, as you know, the outside is crusty.

The crust you are sitting on right now
is rock formed from cooled magma—that hot,
bubbling, gassy mess I told you about.

LAVA

VOLCANO

CRUST

MAGMA

As your planet cooled, the most spectacular thing happened—**water began to collect!**

Oceans formed!

In fact, all of Earth was covered in a shallow ocean. It was very different from all the other planets.

That's when I knew that your Earth was **one of a kind.**

You know what else is special about your planet?

It has life!

I couldn't be prouder.

It all started with little, itty-bitty, teeny-tiny stuff
that lived in that shallow ocean and didn't even
need oxygen. Good thing, too—there wasn't any!

MICROSCOPIC ORGANISMS

I watched as those itty-bitty, teeny-tiny organisms evolved and got even more interesting. New life emerged and used the sun's energy for photosynthesis.

Guess what that produced?

Oxygen!

And all that oxygen, from all those itty-bitty, teeny-tiny life forms, built up in your atmosphere for millions of years.

That is why YOU, Earthling, have oxygen!

I couldn't believe what happened after that. **Life flourished!**

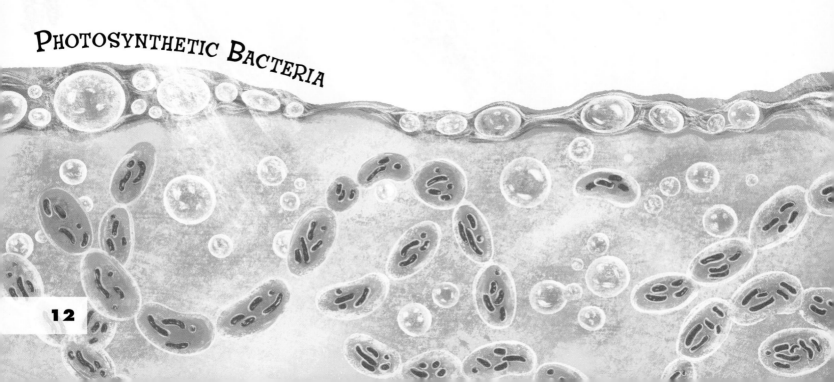

PHOTOSYNTHETIC BACTERIA

13

Plants got bigger.

Animals got bigger—
and more complex.

Creatures developed hard parts such
as shells and spines. Soon, there were
fish, insects, amphibians, reptiles,
dinosaurs, and then mammals.

MERCURY

VENUS

So, why is there life on your
planet but not others? Well,
you've heard the story of *Goldilocks
and the Three Bears*, right?

**Earth is the Goldilocks
of your solar system.**

It's not too close to your sun.

And it's not too far away.

It's just the right distance
so it's **not too hot** and not too cold.

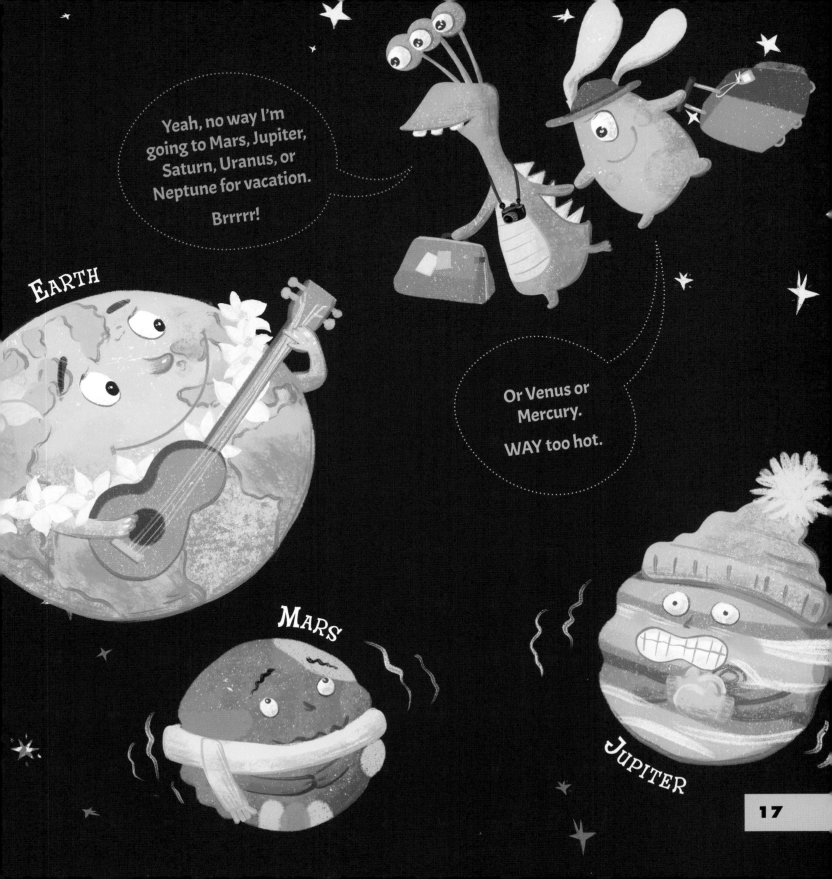

You know what else helps Earth support life? Remember that atmosphere I mentioned? **It's brilliant!**

It works like a shade and a blanket. It protects you and all other life on Earth from the harmful rays of the sun. At the same time, it keeps your planet from getting too cold.

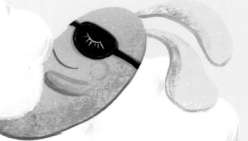

That atmosphere is like a big blanket of gas.

I think they prefer to compare the atmosphere to a greenhouse.

And then there's all the water. Obviously, Earth is no longer covered in a shallow ocean. But 70 percent of the surface of the planet is still covered in liquid water. Thank goodness, because the water in your water cycle is super important to life on Earth.

Including humans!
You know, I'm proud of you humans.

CONDENSATION

EVAPORATION

PRECIPITATION

21

You people are amazing!

Look at all the things you've done. You created
homes and
cities and
cars and
technology.

You've even put a man on the moon!

I can't believe what you've accomplished.

But I'm also sad.

Those humans have come a long way. Now, they have pizza! And cookies! And chocolate ice cream!

Yeah, and to think they used to walk around hunting mastodons with big clubs.

23

All those accomplishments have led to a few problems. These days, your planet is sick.

Feverish.
Smoggy.
Polluted.

And all that life on Earth? It's having a hard time, too. Things are changing too much, too fast. The creatures and the plants and the itty-bitty, teeny-tiny life forms can't adapt. Even the atmosphere is changing.

I'm worried.

25

Yet, I still have hope. Many humans have come up with solutions to help your planet. Many more are already helping! That's what is so smart about you humans. You see a problem and you work hard to fix it.

And I know you will this time, too.

Because Earth is an amazing planet!

27

Make a TERRARIUM

While an aquarium is for fish, a terrarium is for plants. Like Earth, your terrarium will need all the right ingredients in just the right amounts.

The Milky Way

WHAT YOU NEED

a glass container (any size), soil, activated charcoal to work as a water filter (available at an aquarium store), rocks, small plants or seeds, water

WHAT YOU DO

Select plants or seeds that live in the same environment.
For example, cacti like dry environments. Ferns and mosses like wet environments.

Next, layer the materials in the terrarium.
Rocks first. Then charcoal, soil, and finally the seeds or plants. Place the container in a sunny spot.

credit: NASA

Sea turtle

Watch and talk about how well your terrarium plants do.
Don't forget to water as needed. Was it easy or hard to grow the plants? If the plants didn't do well, can you guess why?

Glossary

Aerial view of a rainforest

adapt: to change in order to survive.

amphibian: an animal with moist skin that is born in water but lives on land. Frogs, toads, newts, efts, and salamanders are amphibians.

atmosphere: a blanket of gases around the earth.

bacteria: microbes found in soil, water, plants, and animals that are sometimes harmful but often helpful.

condensation: the process of a gas cooling down and changing into a liquid.

diverse: having lots of different kinds.

evaporation: the process of a liquid heating up and changing into a gas.

evolve: a change in a living thing in response to the world around it.

galaxy: a group of millions or billions of stars. The earth is in a galaxy called the Milky Way.

magma: hot melted rock below the surface of the earth.

mammal: a type of animal, such as a human, dog, or cat. Mammals are born live, feed milk to their young, and usually have hair or fur covering most of their skin.

microbe: a living thing too small to be seen without a microscope.

orbit: the path a planet travels around the sun.

organism: a living thing, such as a plant or animal.

oxygen: a gas in the air that animals and humans need to breathe to stay alive.

photosynthesis: how plants turn sunlight and water into food to grow.

planet: a large body in space that orbits the sun and does not produce its own light. There are eight planets.

pollute: to make dirty.

precipitation: any form of water that falls from clouds.

reptile: an animal covered with scales that crawls on its belly or on short legs. Snakes, turtles, lizards, alligators, and crocodiles are reptiles.

solar system: a family of eight planets and their moons that orbit the sun.

technology: the use of science to invent things or solve problems.

universe: everything that exists, everywhere.

water cycle: the continuous movement of water from the earth to the clouds and back again.

Earth from space

Earthrise from the moon

29

credit: NASA

EXPLORE AWESOME ADAPTATIONS IN THIS PICTURE BOOK SCIENCE SET!

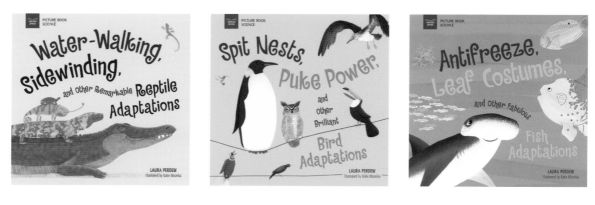

Check out more titles at www.nomadpress.net

Nomad Press

A division of Nomad Communications

10 9 8 7 6 5 4 3 2 1

This book was manufactured by CGB Printers,
North Mankato, Minnesota, United States
March 2021, Job #1018011

ISBN Softcover: 978-1-61930-984-5
ISBN Hardcover: 978-1-61930-981-4

Educational Consultant, Marla Conn

Questions regarding the ordering of this book should be addressed to
Nomad Press
2456 Christian St., White River Junction, VT 05001
www.nomadpress.net

Printed in the United States.